Giant Pandas

by Lynn M. Stone
photographs by Keren Su

Lerner Publications Company • Minneapolis

For Brittany
  —LMS

To my wife, Cecilia, and my daughter, Leanne
                          —KS

The photographs on pp. 8, 17, and 35 are reproduced with the permission of Lynn M. Stone.

Lerner Publications Company
A division of Lerner Publishing Group
241 First Avenue North
Minneapolis, MN 55401 U.S.A.

Website address: www.lernerbooks.com

Library of Congress Cataloging-in-Publication Data

Stone, Lynn M.
    Giant pandas / by Lynn M. Stone ; photographs by Keren Su.
      p.   cm. — (Early bird nature books)
    ISBN: 0–8225–3042–2 (lib. bdg. : alk. paper)
      1. Giant panda—Juvenile literature. [1. Giant panda.
    2. Pandas. 3. Endangered species.] I. Su, Keren, ill. II. Title.
    III. Series.
    QL737.C214 S76 2002
    599.789—dc21   2001001803

Manufactured in the United States of America
1 2 3 4 5 6 – JR – 07 06 05 04 03 02

Contents

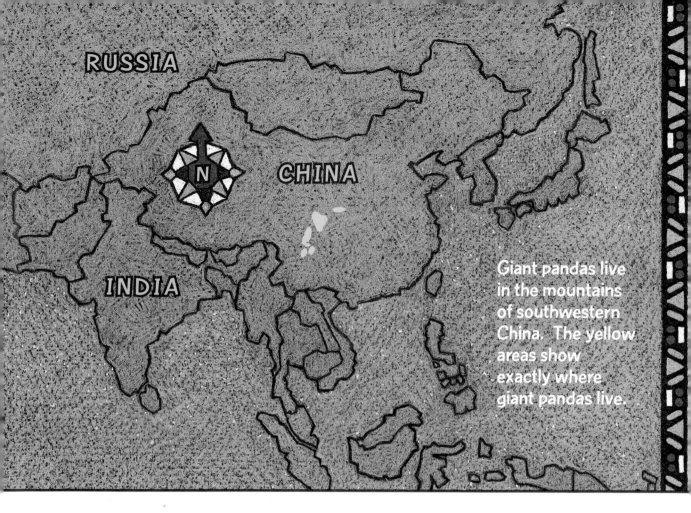

Giant pandas live in the mountains of southwestern China. The yellow areas show exactly where giant pandas live.

Be a Word Detective

Can you find these words as you read about the giant panda's life? Be a detective and try to figure out what they mean. You can turn to the glossary on page 46 for help.

bamboo	habitat	reserves
captive	home range	scent
cubs	nursing	shoots
den	poachers	

Chapter 1

The scientific name of the giant panda is Ailuropoda melanoleuca. Where do giant pandas live?

A Most Unusual Bear

A giant panda looks cute and cuddly, like a teddy bear. But a giant panda is not a toy. It is a wild bear that lives in China.

The giant panda has a large, round head. It has a short, black nose and round ears. Most of the fur on a panda's head is white. But its ears are black. And there is black fur around its eyes. The panda looks like it is wearing a mask!

The giant panda's belly and part of its back are white. But there is black fur on its legs and around its middle. Its short tail looks like a furry, white pancake.

A giant panda is up to 6 feet long from nose to tail. It weighs up to 350 pounds.

In some ways, the giant panda is like other bears. It has a short neck and thick shoulders. It has thick fur. And it has long claws on its paws. A giant panda can stand on its two back paws. But it does not walk upright. Instead, a panda walks on all four feet. The panda swings its head back and forth when it walks.

Grizzly bears are relatives of the giant panda.
These grizzly bears are fishing in a river in Alaska.

Giant pandas can't walk like people. Pandas use all four legs when they walk.

In other ways, the giant panda is a very unusual bear. Most bears roar and growl. But giant pandas whine and make bleating noises, like sheep. Most bears eat only meat or both meat and plants. But the giant panda eats mostly bamboo plants.

Chapter 2

Giant pandas eat mostly bamboo. Is it easy for other kinds of animals to eat bamboo?

The Bamboo Bear

 The Chinese people have a wonderful nickname for the giant panda. They call it the bamboo bear, because it eats so much bamboo.

Bamboo plants have long, stiff stems and narrow leaves. Much of a bamboo plant is crunchy. For most animals, bamboo would be hard to eat. But the giant panda can easily eat bamboo.

Pandas have strong teeth. A panda's side teeth can cut through bamboo stems that are as thick as a man's leg! A panda's throat has a tough lining so the panda isn't hurt by bamboo splinters.

Giant pandas eat the leaves, roots, and shoots of bamboo plants. Shoots are new, leafy plants that grow each spring.

This panda is standing near some bamboo plants. Some kinds of bamboo grow to be very tall.

A giant panda uses its wrist bone to hold a stalk of bamboo.

Bears don't have thumbs. But each of the giant panda's front paws has a special extra "finger." The extra "finger" is really part of the panda's wrist bone. The panda uses the bone like you use your thumb. A giant panda holds bamboo between this "finger" and its paw. It pops one piece of bamboo after another into its mouth.

Giant pandas need to eat lots of bamboo. Bamboo is not rich in vitamins. To stay healthy, a giant panda must eat and eat. It may spend as many as 16 hours each day eating bamboo!

Pandas usually eat bamboo. They also eat other kinds of plants. And sometimes they eat insects, fish, small animals, or birds.

Many kinds of bamboo grow in China. The giant panda's favorite kinds are called arrow bamboo and umbrella bamboo.

There are many different kinds of bamboo plants. Each kind of bamboo grows flowers at a different time. After a bamboo plant grows flowers, it dies. So all of the plants of one kind of bamboo die at the same time. When one kind of bamboo dies off, giant pandas can usually find another kind of bamboo to eat.

Chapter 3

Pandas live on mountains in China. What do we call a panda's home in the wild?

Panda Homes

Bamboo grows well in the mountains of southwestern China. That's where giant pandas

16

live. A panda's home in the wild is called its habitat. Pandas share their habitat with many other animals. Pheasants (FEH-zuhnts), monkeys, bamboo rats, squirrels, takins (TAH-keenz), and snakes all live in the panda's habitat.

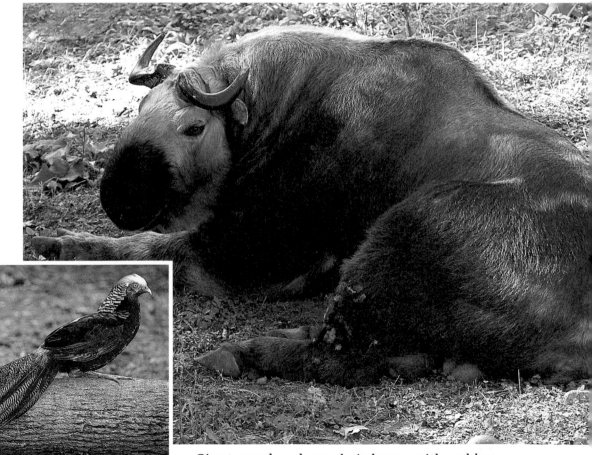

Giant pandas share their home with golden pheasants (left) *and takins* (above).

Scientists found 1,700 different kinds of plants in one forest where pandas live!

The panda's habitat has big, rocky cliffs. But it also has deep green forests. The forests are full of trees, ferns, flowers, shrubs, and bamboo. Brooks rush through the forests and tumble in crashing waterfalls. Low clouds curl around the mountains. Clouds are made up of water. So the clouds often make the panda's habitat foggy and wet. The fog keeps the forest green.

The giant panda's habitat is often foggy.

In the summer, pandas live high in the mountains.

In the summer, the giant panda's habitat is mild in the daytime and cool at night. In the fall, the days become cooler and nights can be frosty. It is colder at the top of the mountains than it is farther down the slopes. So as the weather becomes cooler, the pandas move down the mountains.

In the fall, the leaves of trees in the panda's habitat change color. Pandas begin to move down the mountains.

Wind and snow lash the mountaintops in winter. But by then, the pandas have moved down to lower forests. There, the winter days are chilly, damp, and sometimes snowy. Even in winter, giant pandas can find bamboo to eat. Bamboo stays green all year long.

Even in the winter, bamboo plants stay green.

In the spring, pandas move back up the mountainsides.

In spring, new bamboo shoots grow in the lower parts of the mountains. As the weather becomes warmer, new shoots grow in higher places, too. Giant pandas begin to move up the mountains. They eat bamboo shoots as they go. By the middle of summer, the pandas are once again high in the mountains.

23

Chapter 4

It is hard to see far in the panda's foggy home. How can pandas tell when other pandas are nearby?

Panda Neighborhoods

Each giant panda lives in its own neighborhood in panda habitat. A panda's neighborhood is called its home range. Usually pandas share part of their home range with other pandas. But the pandas rarely see each other.

Pandas can't see well. It's hard for them to see through the thick, foggy bamboo forests.

But pandas know when other pandas are nearby. Each panda makes a smelly liquid called scent (SENT). The panda leaves scent on rocks or trees in its home range. Panda scent wouldn't mean much to a person. But scent means a lot to other pandas.

A panda's scent is like a letter. It tells other pandas whether the scent was left by a male panda or a female panda. It also tells whether the panda is ready to start a family.

Pandas usually live alone. But they can use scent to find out about other pandas.

Chapter 5

A newborn panda is about the size of a chipmunk. How many babies does a mother panda have at one time?

Panda Families

 Baby giant pandas are called cubs. Panda cubs are usually born in September. They are born in a safe place called a den. The den may be a small cave or a space under a tree.

A mother panda usually has one or two cubs at one time. If she has two cubs, she will usually take care of only one of them.

A newborn panda cub weighs just 3 to 5 ounces. That's less than a baseball weighs. The cub is nearly hairless. Its eyes are shut tight.

This baby panda is two weeks old.

This cub is drinking milk from its mother.

The panda mom protects her cub and
keeps it warm. She feeds the cub milk from her
body. Drinking mother's milk is called nursing.

The cub's fur grows quickly. Within four weeks, the youngster has black-and-white fur like its mother's. The cub's eyes open when it is six to nine weeks old.

Mother pandas lick their cubs to clean them.

The mother panda and her cub leave the den when the cub is about six weeks old. The youngster cannot walk yet. So the mother panda carries the cub gently in her mouth. When she eats, the baby rests nearby.

This cub is two months old. It can see, but it can't walk yet.

Giant panda cubs like to play.

The cub begins to walk and play when it is three or four months old. Then the cub can follow its mother. When the cub is five or six months old, it begins to eat bamboo. But the cub still nurses too. When the young panda is about nine months old, it stops nursing. It eats more bamboo. It drinks water from a brook. It learns to climb trees.

This cub is six months old. It can eat bamboo, but it still drinks milk too.

The cub stays with its mother for at least a year and a half. By the time the cub is two years old, it lives on its own.

A giant panda is an adult when it is about six years old. Then it is ready to begin its own family.

A wild giant panda may live to be more than 20 years old. But most wild pandas don't live that long. Pandas who live in zoos may live to be 30 years old.

This cub is one year old. It still lives with its mother.
But soon it will be able to live on its own.

Chapter 6

No animals hunt pandas that are grown up. What animals sometimes kill baby pandas?

Problems for Pandas

Leopards, black bears, and large weasels sometimes kill baby pandas. But these animals can't hurt adult pandas. Wild animals aren't a big problem for pandas, but people are.

Poachers are people who kill wild animals even though it's against the law. It's illegal to hunt giant pandas. But poachers hunt pandas anyway. The poachers make large amounts of money by selling panda bones and body parts.

Legal hunters are another problem. Hunters set traps to catch animals. The hunters do not try to catch pandas. But sometimes their traps catch pandas by mistake.

Sometimes leopards hunt panda cubs.

This woman is working on a farm that is near the giant panda's habitat.

The biggest problem for pandas is that China has many, many people. All of China's people need places to live. They need places to build villages, factories, and farms. People cut down the bamboo forests to build towns and farms. And they cut more trees for firewood.

Much of the panda's habitat has been destroyed. People have crowded pandas into smaller and smaller places. These places are surrounded by towns and farms.

Once this mountain was covered with forests. But people cut down many of the trees to make farms.

These men are scientists. They are looking for giant pandas. They want to find out more about how pandas live.

When the bamboo in one place dies, pandas need to find other places where bamboo is still living. If pandas live in a small forest, they may not be able to find any bamboo that is still alive. And the pandas cannot go to other places where the bamboo is still alive. There are too many miles of villages and farms between the panda forests. Then the pandas starve to death.

China wants to help giant pandas. People are no longer allowed to cut trees in most of the forests where pandas live. And there are places where pandas are protected. These places are called reserves. Most of the panda reserves are too far from one another. So pandas cannot go from one reserve to another. But China may find ways to help pandas travel between the reserves.

Panda reserves are safe places for pandas to live.

Chapter 7

This is a place where people take care of giant pandas. What do we call pandas who do not live in the wild?

The Panda Hotel

 Pandas that don't live in the wild are called captive pandas. Many captive pandas are kept in China and in zoos around the world.

The Wolong Nature Reserve has many wild giant pandas. But it is also the biggest home for captive pandas. In the reserve is a place that is like a panda hotel. Each panda has its own room and a yard to play in. There are hillsides where the pandas can explore, climb, and curl up for naps.

This man is cutting bamboo for captive pandas to eat.

When a baby panda is born at Wolong, scientists watch to make sure the cub stays healthy. If a mother panda has twins, she will not take care of both cubs. Then the scientists raise the other cub themselves.

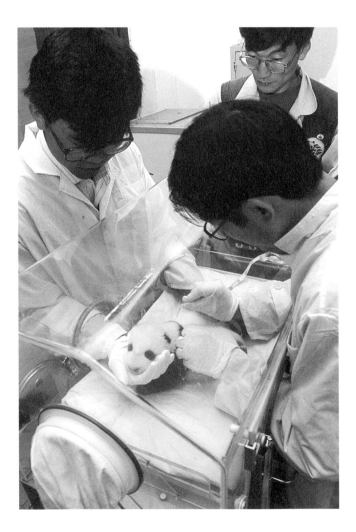

Scientists are checking this baby panda to make sure it is healthy.

People are helping the giant panda. Someday there may be more wild pandas living in China's mountains.

Someday people may be able to release captive pandas back into the wild. Then there would be more wild giant pandas. That would help these unusual bears to always be part of the world's wildlife.

On Sharing a Book

As you know, adults greatly influence a child's attitude toward reading. When a child sees you read, or when you share a book with a child, you're sending a message that reading is important. Show the child that reading a book together is important to you. Find a comfortable, quiet place. Turn off the television and limit other distractions, such as telephone calls.

Be prepared to start slowly. Take turns reading parts of this book. Stop and talk about what you're reading. Talk about the photographs. You may find that much of the shared time is spent discussing just a few pages. This discussion time is valuable for both of you, so don't move through the book too quickly. If the child begins to lose interest, stop reading. Continue sharing the book at another time. When you do pick up the book again, be sure to revisit the parts you have already read. Most importantly, enjoy the book!

Be a Vocabulary Detective

You will find a word list on page 5. Words selected for this list are important to the understanding of the topic of this book. Encourage the child to be a word detective and search for the words as you read the book together. Talk about what the words mean and how they are used in the sentence. Do any of these words have more than one meaning? You will find these words defined in a glossary on page 46.

What about Questions?

Use questions to make sure the child understands the information in this book. Here are some suggestions:

> What did this paragraph tell us? What does this picture show? What do you think we'll learn about next? How are giant pandas like other bears? How are they different? What do pandas eat? Could a giant panda live in your backyard? Why/Why not? What are baby pandas called? How long does a young panda live with its mother? How do people cause problems for giant pandas? What do you think it's like being a panda? What is your favorite part of the book? Why?

If the child has questions, don't hesitate to respond with questions of your own, such as: What do *you* think? Why? What is it that you don't know? If the child can't remember certain facts, turn to the index.

Introducing the Index

The index is an important learning tool. It helps readers get information quickly without searching throughout the whole book. Turn to the index on page 47. Choose an entry, such as *size*, and ask the child to use the index to find out how big a newborn giant panda is. Repeat this exercise with as many entries as you like. Ask the child to point out the differences between an index and a glossary. (The index helps readers find information quickly, while the glossary tells readers what words mean.)

Where in the World?

Many plants and animals found in the Early Bird Nature Books series live in parts of the world other than the United States. Encourage the child to find the places mentioned in this book on a world map or globe. Take time to talk about climate, terrain, and how you might live in such places.

All the World in Metric!

Although our monetary system is in metric units (based on multiples of 10), the United States is one of the few countries in the world that does not use the metric system of measurement. Here are some conversion activities you and the child can do using a calculator:

WHEN YOU KNOW:	MULTIPLY BY:	TO FIND:
miles	1.609	kilometers
feet	0.3048	meters
inches	2.54	centimeters
gallons	3.787	liters
tons	0.907	metric tons
pounds	0.454	kilograms

Activities

Go to the library or visit websites to learn more about giant pandas. The panda websites run by the National Zoo (http://pandas.si.edu/) and the WWF (http://www.panda.org/kids/wildlife/mnpanda.htm) are good places to start.

Pretend to be a giant panda. How do you walk? How do you eat? What sounds do you make?

Make up a story about giant pandas. Be sure to include information from this book. Draw or paint pictures to illustrate your story.

Glossary

bamboo: a kind of grass that has long, stiff stems and narrow leaves. Bamboo is the giant panda's main food.

captive: living with people instead of living in the wild. Many captive animals live in zoos.

cubs: baby giant pandas

den: a safe place where baby pandas are born

habitat: the area where a kind of animal can live and grow

home range: a giant panda's own neighborhood

nursing: drinking mother's milk

poachers: people who kill wild animals even though it's against the law

reserves: places where pandas are protected

scent (SENT): a smelly liquid. Pandas leave scent on rocks and trees as a message for other pandas.

shoots: new, leafy plants that grow in the spring

Index

Pages listed in **bold** type refer to photographs.

About the Author

Lynn M. Stone is an author and photographer who has written more than 250 books for young readers about wildlife and natural history. He is the author and photographer of *Brown Bears*, *Cougars*, *Penguins*, *Sandhill Cranes*, and *Swans*, and the photographer for *Tigers* and *Vultures*, all titles in Lerner's Early Bird Nature Books series. In addition to photographing wildlife, Mr. Stone enjoys fishing and traveling. A former teacher, he lives with his wife and daughter in St. Charles, Illinois.

About the Photographer

Keren Su was born in Hangzhou, China. He is a self-taught photographer, painter, adventurer, and culture explorer. He has bicycled 3,000 miles across China; headed the first rafting expedition down the Tarim, the world's longest interior river; and served as coordinator and guide for the 1990 Peace Expedition to Mt. Everest. Keren has published written and photographic accounts of the lives of Chinese minority peoples, sharing glimpses of many never-before-seen parts of China and the people who live there. He has received numerous awards for his photography of people and nature.